Asteroids

by Gregory L. Vogt

Consultant:
Ralph Winrich
Former NASA Aerospace Education Specialist

Bridgestone Books DISCARD
an imprint of Capstone Press
Mankato, Minnesota

Bridgestone Books are published by Capstone Press
151 Good Counsel Drive, P.O. Box 669, Mankato, Minnesota 56002
http://www.capstone-press.com

Library of Congress Cataloging-in-Publication Data
Vogt, Gregory.
    Asteroids / by Gregory L. Vogt.
    p. cm.—(The galaxy)
    Includes bibliographical references and index.
    Summary: Describes the formation, surface features, and exploration of asteroids,
including the search for near-Earth asteroids.
    ISBN 0-7368-1118-4
    1. Asteroids—Juvenile literature. [1. Asteroids.] I. Title. II. Series.
QB651 .V635 2002
523.44—dc21
        2001003052

Editorial Credits
Tom Adamson, editor; Karen Risch, product planning editor; Timothy Halldin,
    cover designer and interior layout designer; Jenny Schonborn, interior illustrator and
    production designer; Katy Kudela, photo researcher

Photo Credits
Astronomical Society of the Pacific, 10, 14
AURA/STScI/NASA, 18 (top)
JPL/TSADO/TOM STACK & ASSOCIATES, cover, 1, 12
NASA, 20 (bottom)
NASA—Goddard Space Flight Center/JHUAPL/NLR, 6, 20 (top)
NASA/JHUAPL, 8
REUTERS/NASA/Don Davis/Hulton | Archive, 16
StockTrek/PhotoDisc/PictureQuest, 4, 18 (bottom)

1 2 3 4 5 6 07 06 05 04 03 02

Table of Contents

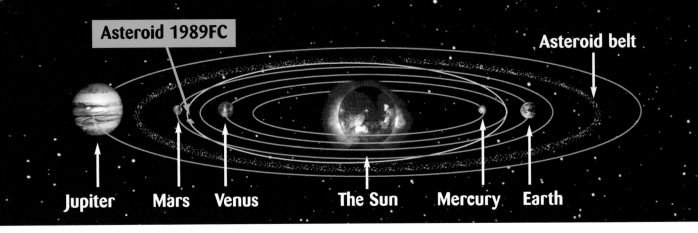

Asteroid 1989FC

Asteroid belt

Jupiter   Mars   Venus   The Sun   Mercury   Earth

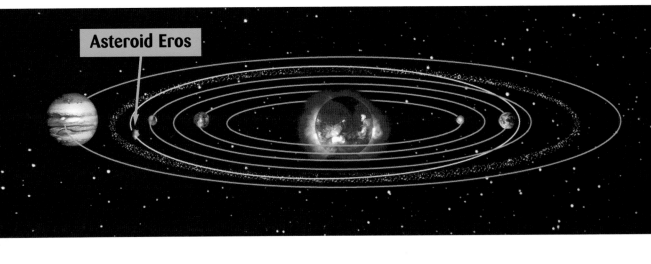

Asteroid Eros

Asteroid Toutatis

What Are Asteroids?

Asteroids are large space rocks that orbit the Sun. But they are too small to be planets. Asteroids are sometimes called minor planets.

Asteroids are leftover pieces from when the solar system formed. The solar system is the Sun and everything that moves around it.

Tens of thousands of asteroids orbit the Sun. Most asteroids travel in a doughnut-shaped belt. The inner edge of the belt is about twice as far from the Sun as Earth is. The outer edge is four times farther away. The asteroid belt is between the orbits of Mars and Jupiter.

Other asteroids are much closer to Earth. These asteroids are called near-Earth asteroids, or NEAs. So far, astronomers have discovered about 800 NEAs. Some of these asteroids cross Earth's orbit.

◀ These illustrations show the orbits of the planets out as far as Jupiter. The asteroid belt is between the orbits of Jupiter and Mars. The orbits of asteroids 1989FC, Eros, and Toutatis are in yellow.

FAST FACTS: The Four Largest Known Asteroids

Name:	Made of:	Average Distance from the Sun:	Diameter:
1. 1 Ceres	Rock and carbon	2.8 AU	584 miles (940 kilometers)
2. 2 Pallas	Rock and carbon	2.7 AU	358 miles (576 kilometers)
3. 4 Vesta	Rock	2.4 AU	329 miles (529 kilometers)
4. 10 Hygeia	Rock and carbon	3.1 AU	267 miles (430 kilometers)
Compared to Earth:			
Earth	Rock and metal	1 AU	7,927 miles (12,756 kilometers)

AU stands for Astronomical Unit. An AU is the distance between Earth and the Sun. One AU is 93 million miles (150 million kilometers).

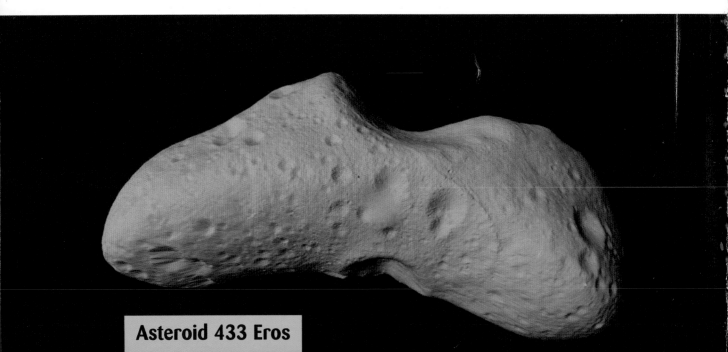

Asteroid 433 Eros

More than 4 billion years ago, the solar system was a giant cloud of gas and dust in space. Gravity brought dust particles closer together.

Most of the cloud formed the Sun. Smaller clumps of gas and dust became the planets and moons. Still smaller clumps were left over after the solar system formed. This leftover material became asteroids.

Thousands of asteroids orbit the Sun. The largest known asteroid is 1 Ceres. It is 584 miles (940 kilometers) across. Asteroid 433 Eros is much smaller. This potato-shaped asteroid is 21 miles (34 kilometers) long. If all known asteroids were combined into a single object, it would be a ball about 930 miles (1,500 kilometers) across. This size is less than half as wide as the Moon.

The number 433 in front of the name Eros means that it is the 433rd asteroid to be discovered. The first asteroid discovered is 1 Ceres.

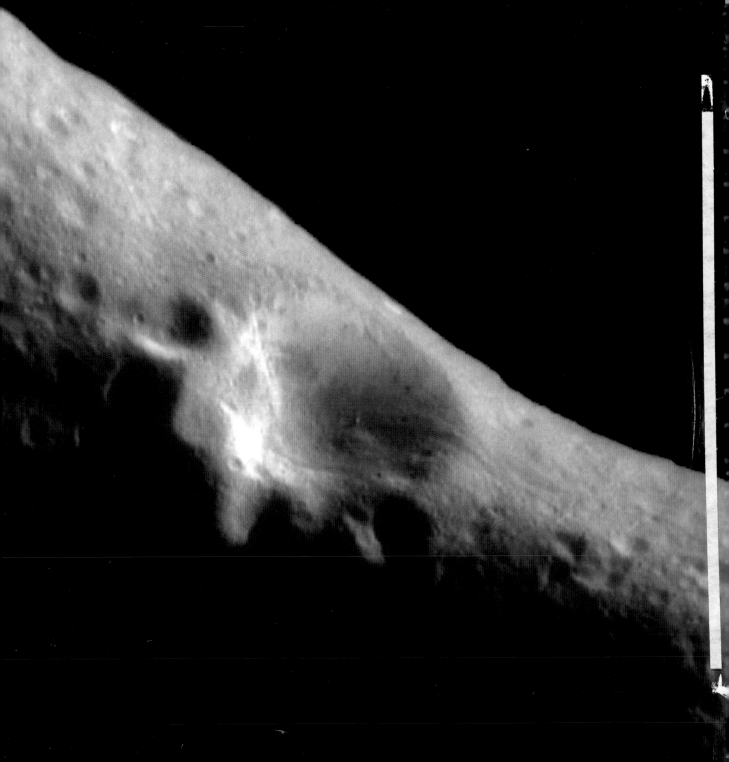

Asteroids are very faint and hard to see. Through a telescope, they look like tiny stars. Stars are far away and appear to stay in the same places. Asteroids are closer to Earth. Each night, astronomers can see asteroids crossing in front of stars.

On February 12, 2001, a space probe landed on asteroid 433 Eros. The space probe was called *Near Earth Asteroid Rendezvous*, or *NEAR*. The space probe orbited Eros for one year before landing on it. *NEAR* used rockets to slow itself and gently touched down. *NEAR* took pictures of Eros as it got closer. It sent the pictures to Earth by radio waves.

Eros is mostly rock mixed with some metal. Its surface is covered with house-sized boulders and small rocks. The surface also has many craters. These holes formed on the asteroid when smaller space rocks crashed into it. Except for size and shape differences, other asteroids probably look similar to Eros.

This large crater on Eros is about 3.3 miles (5.3 kilometers) across. It is named Psyche.

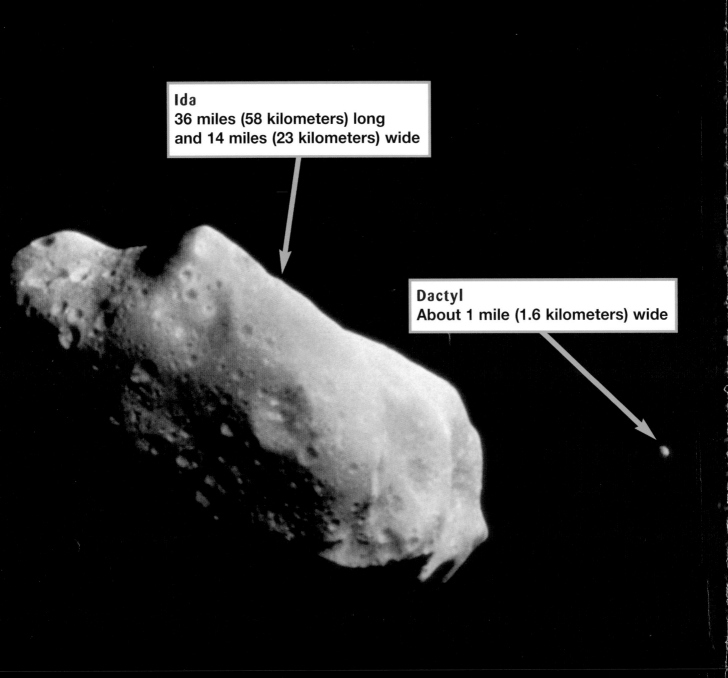

Ida
36 miles (58 kilometers) long
and 14 miles (23 kilometers) wide

Dactyl
About 1 mile (1.6 kilometers) wide

Eros was not the first asteroid to be visited by a space probe. The *Galileo* space probe made the first ever visit to an asteroid. In 1989, *Galileo* was launched on a mission to Jupiter. In 1991, *Galileo* flew by asteroid 951 Gaspra. It took many pictures of the asteroid.

Two years later, *Galileo* flew by asteroid 243 Ida. *Galileo* also sent back pictures of this asteroid. When scientists saw the pictures, they made an important discovery. Ida was not alone.

Scientists saw an even smaller asteroid orbiting Ida about 60 miles (97 kilometers) away. Astronomers wondered if asteroids could have their own moons. Ida and its moon proved it was possible. Ida's moon is now called Dactyl. Astronomers think many other asteroids also may have moons.

Galileo took this photo of Ida and its small moon Dactyl.

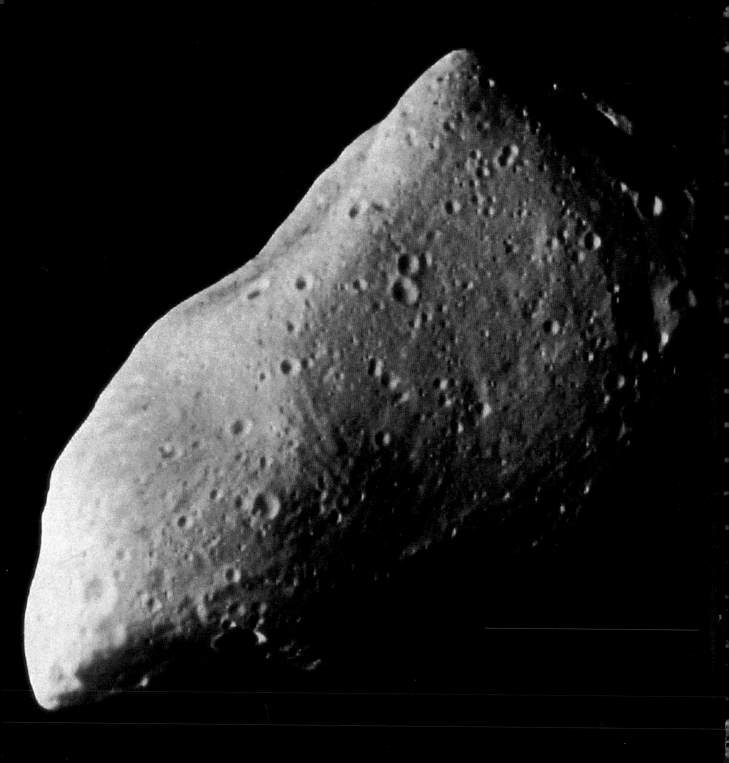

When Asteroids Collide

Tens of thousands of asteroids orbit the Sun. Most asteroids stay far apart from one another. They each follow their own orbits.

An asteroid sometimes gets close to the planet Jupiter. Jupiter's powerful gravity can change the asteroid's orbit. Jupiter's gravity may send the asteroid closer to the Sun. The asteroid also may collide with another asteroid.

The collision may be small if the two asteroids are heading in the same direction. But the crash could be powerful if they hit head-on. The smaller asteroid can be destroyed. The bigger one is left with a large crater.

When asteroids collide, the broken asteroid pieces scatter in all directions. Some pieces could reach Earth. When they do, they streak through the sky and land on the ground. The asteroid piece then is called a meteorite. Meteorites can be pebbles or rocks the size of buildings.

This *Galileo* photo of Gaspra shows that its surface is covered with craters. Scientists added color to the photo to make the craters easier to see.

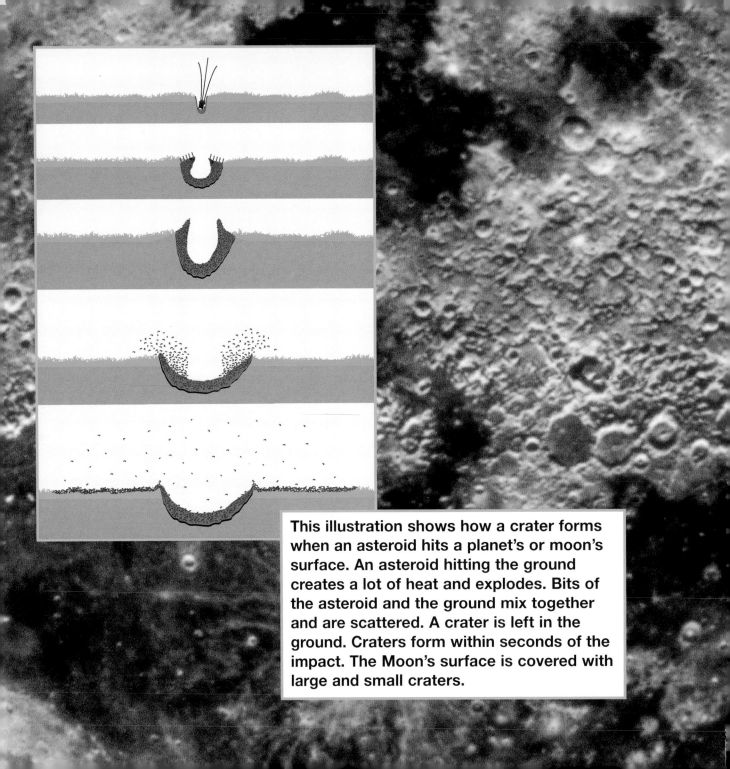

This illustration shows how a crater forms when an asteroid hits a planet's or moon's surface. An asteroid hitting the ground creates a lot of heat and explodes. Bits of the asteroid and the ground mix together and are scattered. A crater is left in the ground. Craters form within seconds of the impact. The Moon's surface is covered with large and small craters.

Impact Craters

Astronomers have discovered that the rocky planets and most moons have impact craters. Many craters are hundreds of miles across.

Impact craters formed when asteroids struck the rocky planets and moons. The impacts cause huge explosions. Millions of tons of rock are crushed into dust. The dust is thrown into the air.

A large crater is formed on the surface. A high rim is pushed upward. Layers in the rock are bent upward like a large blister.

On Earth, wind and water wear away craters. On some planets and moons, the craters last a long time. People can see many giant craters on Earth's Moon. These round dark areas are visible during a full Moon.

Giant planets such as Jupiter also have been hit by asteroids. But craters do not form on these planets. These planets are made of gases. The holes made by the asteroids fill in quickly.

Many scientists think Earth was changed when an asteroid struck 65 million years ago. Dinosaurs such as Brachiosaurus and Tyrannosaurus rex roamed Earth at that time.

A 6-mile-wide (10-kilometer-wide) asteroid was on a collision course with Earth. The asteroid roared through Earth's atmosphere. It slammed into the ground where the country of Mexico is today.

The explosion probably triggered earthquakes, huge waves, and fires. Millions of tons of rock and dust were thrown into the air. The rock and dust blocked the Sun for several months. Earth's air became bad to breathe. The ocean waters were poisoned.

In time, the Sun came out again. But 70 percent of all the life on Earth was dead. The large dinosaurs were now extinct.

Scientists think that a large asteroid struck Earth near Mexico 65 million years ago. It may have caused the dinosaurs to become extinct.

Name an Asteroid

An asteroid may appear as a streak of light in a telescope picture. The person who discovers an asteroid gets to name it. The asteroid first goes by a temporary name. For example, 2001BF means the asteroid was discovered in the year 2001. The B means it was discovered in the second half of January. The second letter tells how many other asteroids were discovered before that one. 2001BF was the sixth asteroid discovered in the second half of January.

Earth

Moon

1989FC

Asteroid Hunting

On March 23, 1989, asteroid 1989FC came close to Earth. This small asteroid is about .25 mile (.4 kilometer) wide. It was traveling about 46,000 miles (74,000 kilometers) per hour. The asteroid missed Earth by about twice the distance to the Moon. The asteroid passed the same point Earth had been six hours before.

Some astronomers around the world hunt for asteroids. They are looking for asteroids similar to 1989FC. They use telescopes to take pictures of the sky. A small, faint streak in a picture could be an asteroid.

Using computers, astronomers compare the streak to known asteroids. Most likely, the asteroid already is known. But the streak sometimes is a new asteroid. Astronomers name it and calculate its orbit. Astronomers discover about 30 asteroids every month.

This illustration shows the relative distance of asteroid 1989FC's close approach to Earth in March 1989.

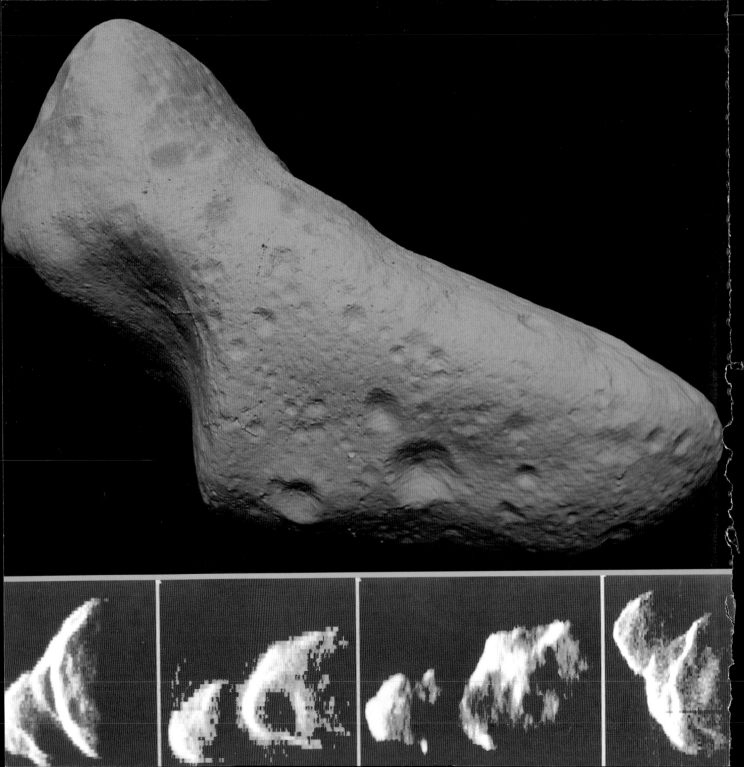

Scientists are searching for more NEAs that may come close to Earth. Astronomers can try to protect Earth if they think an asteroid may hit the planet. First, they will find the exact location of the asteroid. Scientists can send rockets to the asteroid. The rockets will carry atomic bombs. The rockets will approach the asteroid and orbit the asteroid.

The bombs would not blow up the asteroid. Instead, they would explode near it. This explosion would change the path of the asteroid. Blowing up the asteroid might cause it to break into thousands of large boulders. These large rocks would still hit Earth and cause damage. The bombs would shove the asteroid into a different orbit. Earth would be safe.

Eros (above) and Toutatis (below) are NEAs. Toutatis sometimes crosses Earth's orbit.

Hands On: Impact!

Asteroids sometimes collide and form craters. You can see what happens when craters form.

What You Need

Shallow aluminum foil tray
Sand
Flour
Small stones

What You Do

1. Do this activity outside. Cover the bottom of the tray with sand.
2. Sprinkle a thin layer of flour over the sand.
3. Pour another layer of sand and cover it with flour. Add another layer of sand and flour. The tray should be filled almost to the top.
4. Hold a stone high above the sand and drop it. Watch what happens to the sand.
5. For a greater effect, throw another stone into the sand. Make sure no one is near the tray when you throw. Again, look at what happens to the sand.

The stones will form craters. Dark sand will spray out over the white flour.

Words to Know

astronomer (uh-STRON-uh-mer)—a person who studies planets, stars, and space

crater (KRAY-tur)—a hole in the ground made by a meteorite

extinct (ek-STINGKT)—no longer living anywhere in the world; scientists think dinosaurs became extinct 65 million years ago after an asteroid hit Earth.

gravity (GRAV-uh-tee)—a force that pulls objects together

impact (IM-pakt)—the striking of one object against another

meteorite (MEE-tee-ur-rite)—a piece of space rock that strikes a planet or a moon

orbit (OR-bit)—the path of an object as it moves around another object in space

telescope (TEL-uh-skope)—an instrument that makes faraway objects appear larger and closer

Read More

Bonar, Samantha. *Asteroids.* Watts Library. New York: Franklin Watts, 1999.

Gallant, Roy A. *Comets, Asteroids, and Meteorites.* Kaleidoscope. Tarrytown, N.Y.: Benchmark Books, 2001.

Vogt, Gregory. *Asteroids, Comets, and Meteors.* Our Universe. Austin, Texas: Steadwell Books, 2001.

Useful Addresses

Canadian Space Agency
6767 Route de l'Aéroport
Saint-Hubert, QC J3Y 8Y9
Canada

The Planetary Society
65 North Catalina Avenue
Pasadena, CA 91106-2301

Internet Sites

Near Earth Asteroid Rendezvous
http://near.jhuapl.edu/NEAR
The Nine Planets—The Asteroid Belt
http://www.staq.qld.edu.au/k9p/asteroid.htm
Solar System Collisions
http://janus.astro.umd.edu/astro/impact.html

Index